GLORY ROAD
The Life and Times of a Wannabe

By Teddy Lee

Published by New Generation Publishing in 2014

Copyright © Teddy Lee 2014

First Edition

The author asserts the moral right under the Copyright, Designs and Patents Act 1988 to be identified as the author of this work.

All Rights reserved. No part of this publication may be reproduced, stored in a retrieval system or transmitted, in any form or by any means without the prior consent of the author, nor be otherwise circulated in any form of binding or cover other than that which it is published and without a similar condition being imposed on the subsequent purchaser.

www.newgeneration-publishing.com

New Generation Publishing

GLORY ROAD
The Life and Times of a Wannabe

Foreword

You should write a book!

How many times have we all heard that over the years?

But that's exactly what my good friend Andy said after I told him a true funny story. So thanks Andy!

I would also like to thank two agents who have been reliable and helpful over the years: First is the Screenlite Agency, so thanks to Carlie, Noel and Kerry. Second is the Ray Knight Agency so thanks also to Ray, Tony and all the happy girls in that office.

And thanks also to friends and family. The biggest thanks has to go to my partner Kate for showing the patience of a saint.

But my reason for writing this book is purely personal... I know very little about the life of my own parents, other than what I witnessed myself.

So hopefully this book will give my family, relatives and friends an insight into my life.

GLORY ROAD
The Life and Times of a Wannabe

What makes someone a wannabe?

Well I think I will let others deicide but in the 1950's I auditioned for Carroll Levis "Discoveries", in the sixties for Hughie Green's "Opportunity Knocks", in the seventies for ITV's "New Faces" and in recent times for "Britain's Got Talent".

So does that make me a wannabe?

There was no such word in my young days. There were no kids that went to stage school. I doubt if such schools existed, certainly not in Middlesbrough. We had sing songs in our house – most of my brothers and sisters would do a turn (as they called it).

Anyway let's do a Julie Andrews and start at the very beginning..

So I was born at a very early age... my mother was with me at the time... and there was a little village called wedlock... and I was born just outside.

"No Teddy no," those old jokes didn't work when you were doing stand up so don't go using them now.

OK... ok so let's move on to my teenage years.

Chapter 1
How it All Started

I was eighteen, happy, a bit drunk and taking a pee in the bathroom. Mum and Dad were in bed, I knew that because Dad's fag end was floating around in the toilet bowl. That told me he was in bed and Mum always went to bed first and pretended to be asleep. That was her idea of contraception. Nine kids in the family, who could blame her?

Anyway, I was happy because I'd been for a drink with a lad I'd worked with in the steel works. Jonny Mac, the modern jazz singer he called himself. Looking back, he was a right nutcase. Anyway, he'd filled my head with his tales of singing in the clubs in Leeds. So that was our plan, to go to Leeds early the next morning.

Right, time for me to go to bed. I opened the bedroom door in the darkness so as not to wake my older brother Bernard and younger brother Bill. They slept in a double bed and I had a single bed close by. Bernard was a light sleeper and he also had a quick temper and could whack me over the head without getting out of bed, which he often did if I woke him, especially if he was on the early shift the next morning. Getting up at five o clock to go to Dorman and Long steelworks was not the best start to anyone's day. But I had managed to get into bed without disturbing anyone and was happy and excited with my thoughts of fame and success in Leeds. I thought I'll just have a quiet little fart before I go to sleep. Whoops it turned out to be a loud and long fart.

I heard Bernard's voice, "You dirty sod, you've farted"

I knew what was coming next... THE WHACK.

Then I heard Dad's voice from the other bedroom

"Will you lot be quiet in there, I've got to be up early in the morning"

Dad's occupation: he was a crane driver and a breeder of children. I fell asleep dreaming of my fame and fortune in Leeds. Bring it on!

I woke the next morning and the house was quiet. Everyone had gone to work. Mum must have gone to the shops or to church, her being a good catholic, hence the nine kids. I got myself ready and had packed my suitcase when the door opened. Mum came in, prayer book in one hand, a packet of fags in the other.

"Stick the kettle on our Teddy. I'm dying for a cup of tea and a fag."

She looked at me and then at my suitcase.

"What's all this, you going somewhere?"

I explained what my intentions were. She did not seem greatly concerned. That surprised me. All she said was,

"What about your job, you're supposed to be working the night shift tonight."

"Jonny Mac's brother is going to tell them we've gone to Leeds" I replied.

"Right, then I'll stick the kettle on myself" she said.

I left the house feeling a bit disappointed at Mum's lack of concern about me leaving. No big deal, just "Bye". I love my mother dearly and have done all my life but how do you get inside the mind of a woman who has given birth to nine children, two of them had died; Veronica aged two and Peter aged six.

Anyway, push on Teddy. So I started to walk across the fields, a shortcut to South Bank area where Jonny Mac lived. It took me about 30 minutes to get to 28

Gold Street. I knocked on the door and a very tall and aggressive woman opened it. She looked down at me, me being only 5 foot 5 inches.

"What do you want?" she barked.

"I've called for Jonny," I mumbled, "we're going to Leeds."

"He's still in bed," she said abruptly "and he's going nowhere."

And immediately she shut the door on my bewildered face. I stood there sad, disappointed and dumbfounded.

"Now what," I thought.

Back across the fields to Mum and the nightshift at Dorman and Long steelworks... all Mum said when I got back home was,

"That was quick, what happened!"

I eventually left the steelworks and got a day job at Smiths Dock Shipyards where I met another lad who liked to sing in the local pubs. His name was Bill.

We started learning songs together in our lunch break. Eventually we bought a couple of straw hats, matching jumpers and slacks. Bill was a better singer and I had the ideas for bits of comedy. We soon started to get paid for our act and over the months we became very popular.

Teddy and Bill rehearsing in their lunchbreak.

Bill and I decided to go for an audition for Carroll Levis "Discoveries" which was being held at the local Variety Theatre. I was late calling round at Bill's house and when we got to the theatre there was a massive queue outside.

We stood in that queue for hours only to be told they would not be doing any more auditions. We were both bitterly disappointed and Bill said it was all my fault because I was late. I've known my mate Bill all my adult life, he's normally very laid back and rarely loses his temper but he did that day and he threw our two straw hats into the middle of a busy road and they were crushed into small pieces by a number nine bus.

But that's show business folks!

Sadly it all came to an end when Bill was called up to do his national service in the Army. We both vowed to continue with the act when he came out.

I had failed my medical for national service due to a bad skin disease that had plagued me for years.

Anyway I had been enjoying our little burst of fame in the local pubs and clubs and was missing it so I decided to buy a guitar and take some lessons.

Chapter 2
Going to Blackpool

I was fed up with my job in the shipyards and one day while I was taking tea break in the bowels of a half built ship, one old worker said,

"Yes I've spent forty years working in these shipyards and I don't regret one minute of it"

I thought right, I don't want my life to start and end in Middlesbrough. So like bucket of prawns in the sun, I was off (that's an Australian joke).

So I got off the train at Blackpool with my suitcase, guitar that I couldn't tune and my post office savings book with £50 in it. I put my suitcase and guitar in one of the lockers at the station and went to the toilet. I was taking a pee when a little man stood next to me.

"Are you looking for digs?" he said.

Not an ideal situation to strike up a conversation with another male but I said,

"Yes I am as a matter of fact"

He took me along the famous Golden Mile, as it was then known to a back street fish shop.

"You stay here, I'll just go and talk to the owner" he said.

He entered the shop and I was starting to get suspicious. A short while later he waved me in. This big fat man came from behind the counter, he'd obviously been eating too many of his own chips.

"I hear you're looking for a place to stay" he said to me in a broad Irish accent.

"Yes" I replied "but I need to see the room first."

"Ahh, it's a lovely room son, you'll be alright here. You just nip off and get your suitcase."

But I insisted on seeing the room so he took me upstairs to a large room with about six single beds crammed into it. Needless to say I left with the little man following me.

I saw a sign down one of the side streets with "vacancy" written on it. I knocked on the door and was shown a nice room on the first floor which I decided to take. I left the landlady a deposit, picked up my gear and got rid of the little man.

I got myself a job in Jenkinson's restaurant as a kitchen porter all in the space of my first day.

"How good am I!"

My happiness was short-lived as regards my nice room because as the summer season progressed, the Blackpool landlady moved me up into the attic. When it got busier, she moved me to the washhouse in the back yard which had no window and a double mattress on the floor. But all the vacancy signs had come down now so I had nowhere else to go.

It got even worse because, at the height of the season, she moved her 22 year old son into the washhouse to share my double mattress. It was a hot night. This big lump of a lad was snoring his head off and I was feeling hot and sweaty.

Remember there were no windows in the washhouse so I got up and opened the door slightly to let some air in and crept back onto the double mattress next to the incredible hulk who was snoring even louder now that we had some fresh air in the washhouse.

I pulled the pillow over my face to drown out his loud snoring and started to count sheep. I got to four hundred and eighty seven and the snoring had stopped. I felt a movement on the pillow and my whole body went rigid. I thought if he tries to kiss me I'm going to knee him right in the bollocks. I felt another movement and this time it was near my private parts. I threw the pillow to one side and sat bolt upright. A big black and white cat gave a little squeal and jumped off the mattress. It scarpered back out of the washhouse door and disappeared into the night. I took a while to compose myself.

Eventually I pulled the pillow over my face and started to count sheep again. Four hundred and eighty eight, four hundred and eighty nine. Oh no, he's started to snore again.

I'm sure not all Blackpool landladies were like the one I got lumbered with but I was about to meet my Mother Theresa in the form of Mrs Fairs, the nicest, kindest, happiest little old lady I've ever met.

I was sat in this working men's club, I'd had a few pints and decided to get up and sing which went down well and I got a big round of applause. As I sat down next to this sweet little lady, she said.

"That was very nice son. Earnest and I really enjoyed it." Earnest was her husband, he smiled and gave me the thumbs up sign.

A few drinks later and I had told the nice lady about all my accommodation problems, she turned to Earnest who was a quite a few pints in and said,

"Teddy can come and stay at our house. He can have our Zoe's old room, couldn't he Earnest?"

"Yeah, why not" said Earnest, picking up his pint.

So the deal was done, She gave me a piece of paper with her name and address plus instructions on how to get there.

"Just bring your stuff around and everything will be fine," she said.

The next day being Sunday, there was no work as the restaurant was closed. I turned up at Mrs Fairs house, 37 Rectory Road with my suitcase and guitar which I still could not bloody tune. I knocked on the door and it opened to reveal Earnest. What I did not know about Earnest was that when he was drinking he was everybody's friend but when he was sober he was a grumpy old sod. He looked down at me with my guitar and suitcase and his first words were,

"Ohh, bloody hell no..."

But he was pushed to one side by my little friend Bet, as she liked me to call her.

"Come in", she said with a big smile. "I'll show you your room."

I looked down at this lovely little lady with a smile bigger than Blackpool and I knew I was going to be fine.

I wrote earlier about my problems of a skin disease which affected me badly in my teenage years. I recall going to a skin specialist and was told to go into a curtained off area of the clinic and remove all my clothes. My arms, legs and parts of my body were covered in weeping sores. When the specialist came to see me his first remarks were,

"Oh dear... we are in a bit of a state aren't we..."

Not a very professional thing to say to a young teenage sensitive boy.

The problem stayed with me until the age of twenty one, not an ideal situation for contact with the opposite sex.

I recall I would lock myself in the bathroom, putting on ointment and bandaging my arms and legs from top to bottom. I remember one very embarrassing experience. I had gone to the local dance and it was the last waltz. I had asked the girl I was dancing with if I could take her home and she had said yes so I was feeling good about myself until I felt a kind of tug at the bandage on my right leg. I looked down behind me to see about 5 yards of bandage trailing me around the dance floor much to the amusement of most of the other couples present. I made my apologies to the nice girl I was dancing with, gathered up the 5 yards of bandage and shot off to the gents toilet. Needless to say when I returned the nice girl had gone, never to be seen again.

"Ah well, not tonight Teddy, better luck next time."

So let's get back to Blackpool. Everything was going fine for me. My skin problems had gone, my digs were great and Mrs Fairs was a dream of a landlady, even Earnest had taken a shine to me because we found we both liked football and boxing.

My job at Jenkinson's restaurant was going well because I was a good young willing worker. They gave me a pay rise and promoted me from kitchen porter to assistant cook. Even my love life took a turn for the better and I finally lost my virginity.

Let me explain. I went to the famous Tower Ballroom and met this very attractive woman called Tina. We had a dance then went to the bar and had a few drinks. We laughed a lot and she asked me what job I did. In an effort to impress Tina I told her I was an electrician. We left the dance together and walked down to the beach. It was a nice warm evening and we kissed under the pier. She had told me earlier in the bar she was a divorced woman with two young children, ideal for a young virgin boy like me. We laid down on the sand and finally I felt like a man... So thanks Tina!

Tina (on the left) and friend.

We saw each other for the rest of the season, her mum and dad had this large house on South Shore. Her and the two children were staying there with them. She arranged for me to go round one morning while the children were at school and her mum and dad were at work. I was lying in this nice double bed and Tina came back into the room carrying this electric toaster (remember I told her I was an electrician).

"This toaster is broken, I wonder if you could fix it for me?"

Lies come back to haunt you. How embarrassed was I? So I gave it a little shake.

"No, you're going to need a new one, the element's gone" I replied.

I have some nice memories of Blackpool. This is another one. I was in this very exclusive night club frequented by top celebrities. The only reason I got in was because I knew the doorman. Standing at the bar was Brian London, the heavyweight champion of Great Britain. Among the group of people he was with was Alma Cogan, a very popular singing star with several songs in the charts at the time.

I walked over to Brian London, turned to Alma Cogan, who was quite a tall girl, and said,

"Could I have this dance please?"

They both looked down at me and smiled.

"What's your name" she said.

I said "Teddy."

She replied "Yes Teddy, I'd love to have a dance with you."

I found her to be a charming and delightful girl. At the end of the dance she wished me luck, went back to the British heavyweight champion and left me with a nice memory of Blackpool.

My time in Blackpool was great. I grew as a person because of the different experiences I had to deal with. I left Jenkinson's Restaurant with a glowing reference. The girl in the office who typed the reference knew of my intentions of going to Manchester and suggested I get in touch with her brother who had a market stall in the city centre. She gave me a letter of introduction with his name written on the front of the envelope together with instructions on how to find him.

I had made a lot of friends at the restaurant. One of my jobs there was to serve on the hotplate which was on the same level as the restaurant. You served all the veg, chips and roast potatoes from the hotplate. This was all cooked on the floor above together with all the other food and was sent down on the dumb waiter, as it was called. You pulled on a rope which brought the hot food down a hatch from the kitchen above and you pulled on the rope again to send it back up for more food. Normally when it got busy, it took two persons to run the hotplate but "our little Teddy" (as the waitresses called me) could manage all on his own.

One of my friends at the restaurant was Tom the kitchen porter. I can only describe Tom as a bit of a tramp. I knew he was sleeping rough but that seemed to be his way of life and had been for many years. But he was a wise and thoughtful man when you got to know him and I couldn't help but like him. Sometimes at the end of the day when the kitchen staff had gone home and Tom was left with a pile of pots, pans and dishes, I would stop back and help him. In his younger days he had travelled the world in the Royal Navy and was an excellent story teller. I valued his wisdom and friendship. When we finally shook hands as I was on my way to Manchester he said,

"If you come unstuck when you get there, go to the Salvation Army hostel. You'll always get a bed there son."

Needless to say I had to do just that but there lies a story for the future. What I will reveal about my friend Tom was that some three years on I was doing well for myself in London and had just bought a brand new car. I was driving over Westminster Bridge in the busy morning traffic when I saw this tramp walking towards me. He was laden down with the usual plastic bags and with Big Ben in the background. The tramps face came closer and lo and behold, it was Tom! The traffic had stopped momentarily and I tooted my horn to attract his attention but to no avail. My old friend Tom was soon lost in the crowd never to be seen again and I had to move on with the busy morning traffic.

Anyway let's get back to my final days in Blackpool. Saying goodbye to Mrs Fairs was sad especially as she had been trying to find me a job so I could stay on through the winter. On the day I left, this happy little lady sat down at her piano and sang that Gracie Field song,

"Wish me luck as you wave me good bye..."

I can still see her face, hear her voice to this day... Goodbye Blackpool, hello Manchester.

Chapter 3
Manchester

It was dark and foggy, my feet were aching from tramping round Manchester looking for digs. I had arrived at midday and called into the Labour Exchange, now known as the Job Centre. They couldn't offer me a job until I had somewhere to stay. They gave me a list of addresses but I had drawn a blank on every one. I also checked out the market stall in the City Centre... but to no avail. My last resort was the Salvation Army Hostel or the doss house as it was commonly known.

I looked at the address Tom had given me and in his wisdom he had written down their telephone number. I rang from the nearest phone box only to be told they did not admit anybody after 10pm. It was now 10.30pm. All the pubs closed at 10 pm. Where was I to go?

I retraced my steps back to a scrap yard, crawled through a gap in the fence and dossed down in a broken old van with no doors on it. Good night Manchester!

Out of bad comes good as many years later this experience prompted me to write a song called "Homeless" and the words go like this....

"Homeless"

> I packed my grip when I was a lad
> And I moved down to London town
> I sang my songs in all the bars
> But a pretty girl I never have found
> They said home is where you make it lad
> Those streets will be paved with gold

> But as I rest my heard on this cardboard pillow
> I cry and I want to go home
> My dreaming days seem over now
> Maybe my time is through
> I've missed the warmth of those pretty girls
> And the love they say is true
> I'm nobody's hero not even their clown
> So I drink to ease my mind
> As I lay here alone on the ground
> I'll pack my grip just one more time
> And I'll move out of London town
> To the friends I knew when I was a lad
> I wonder if they'll understand
> I wonder if they'll understand

The next day I checked into the Salvation Army Hostel and paid my seven and six. That's about 80p in today's money. The man in charge looked at my suitcase and guitar.

"You'll be tempting fate bringing that in here son," he said "you'd better give it to me and I'll lock it away for you."

He pointed towards a door with a long queue outside.

"That's the TV room. It doesn't open till six o'clock. And down the corridor there is the kitchen."

Coming out of the kitchen and walking along the corridor towards me was the scruffiest looking tramp I had ever seen. Long hair, long beard, long dirty black coat. He was carrying an old pan full of steaming hot bones with a little 3 legged dog hopping along behind him. For a moment I thought I was on the film set of "Oliver Twist".

The sleeping arrangements were a long room with cubicles just wide enough to fit a single bed in. I spent two of the most unpleasant nights of my life there.

I eventually found a bed-sit which had a shared kitchen but this was my third day and I had still not found a job. After paying my rent and buying some groceries I went into the kitchen to make a coffee and met a pleasant man who shook my hand, smiled at me and said,

"Hello, my name is John Daily, I've got the bed-sit next to yours."

I told him I had just arrived from Blackpool and was looking for work.

This chirpy happy-go-lucky man was just the type to lift me out of my disillusioned state of mind.

"Do you think you could sell vacuum cleaners?" he said.

"I don't know," I replied "I've never sold anything before."

The next day he took me to his office where I met his manager, a charming Irish man who had a real gift for selling. He shook my hand, looked me up and down and said,

"I'll tell you what son, that baby face of yours will get you in the door and that's the hard bit when you are selling vacuum cleaners."

He turned out to be right because the first door I knocked on, I was invited in to give a demonstration. The selling point of this was to empty the contents of the dustbag onto a white sheet of paper to show how good the cleaner worked.

"You'll be surprised at the amount of dirt this machine will get out of your carpet," I said "and with dirt and dust comes germs and you don't want that in a nice house like this, especially with your little daughter there."

The little girl had been watching my demonstration while happily gurgling away in her high chair. At this point I turned the dustbag upside down onto the white sheet of paper... to reveal.. nothing! No dust, no dirt, no germs. The room went embarrassingly quiet, even the baby had stopped gurgling. The silence was broken by the lady saying,

"Never mind son, would you like a cup of tea and a biscuit?"

"No" I mumbled back, "I'd better get off".

I quickly packed everything back in the box including my pristine sheet of white paper and left.

Later, back in the van, my supervisor could not believe I had got no dirt out of the carpet. He took the cleaner out of the box and said,

"Right... show me what you did?"

I picked up the hose and started to fit it to the cleaner.

"Right, stop there" he said "is that how you did it in the house?"

"Yes" I replied.

"That's the wrong end son... no wonder you got no dirt out of her carpet, you had the hose on the blowing end!"

Oh dear, I thought. Not a good way to start my career as a vacuum cleaner salesman. However let's fast forward a few months. It was Christmas time and I was going home for the Christmas holiday a very happy lad because the firm had held a competition to see who could sell the most vacuum cleaners and guess who beat all the other salesmen. Yes it was... little Teddy Lee! I'm not sure if it was because I was a good salesman or people just felt sorry for me. I'd like to think it was a combination of both.

Anyway I arrived home with my prize, a Christmas hamper and the biggest fattest turkey I'd ever seen. My mother's first remark was,

"Will it fit in the oven, our Teddy?"

Her second remark after it was cooked was,

"My goodness, we'll never eat all that!"

But that night we had a party and a good old sing song. Everyone did a turn but the best turn of the night was "the turkey" because all that was left of it was a big skeleton with not a scrap of flesh to be seen.

And a merry Christmas was had by all.

Back in Manchester after Christmas, the weather did not lend itself to walking the streets selling vacuum cleaners. It was cold, wet and foggy. I recall one night going to the cinema only to find the fog had got in there so everyone was sat at the front to see the action on the screen. In those days people were burning coal, the smokeless coal was not available then. As a result all the major towns and cities had a lot of foggy winters.

My next job was in the packing department of a mail order firm. By this time my old mate Bill had come out of the army and wanted to join me in Manchester so I got him a bedsit in the same house as me and picked him up at the station. As the days progressed I realized he did not want to re-form our double act which I found disappointing. His new ambition was to be a band singer. I can't say I enjoyed the rest of the winter so it was,

"Goodbye Manchester, Hello Jersey"

Chapter 4
Hello Jersey

In those days people took holidays at home more and Jersey had become very popular. Bill and I had read in the national press that the ratio was five girls to every bloke there so we both thought,

"Right, we'll have some of that mate!"

We got the train to Weymouth and across on the boat to Jersey...

"Yippeee... bring on the girls..."

But I think not because the season hadn't started yet and all we found were a lot of horny young men who had read the same newspaper we had. Consequently all the local "ugly betty's" were having a whale of a time.

But looking back, my summer in Jersey was one of the best ever. When the season started, there were lots of good looking girls around and plenty of work for everyone. My first job was in a warehouse grading and packing potatoes. When that season ended I got a job in the gasworks digging up the roads. When the tomato season started I went back to my job in the warehouse, this time grading and packing tomatoes.

I met a great group of lads from the Battersea area of London and we had some great times on the beach having parties and playing football.

Jersey crowd on the beach.

The nightlife in Jersey was terrific. Every hotel had cabaret and some had what they called "crazy nights" where you had to play daft games like girls would dress up as men and the lads would dress up as women.

They were always great fun. One night in the early part of the season Bill and I had gone to Swanson's Hotel to watch the cabaret. On the show were two nice looking girls called "The Brett sisters". We chatted them up and went for a drink with them after the show. I kept in touch with the one I was with right until the end of the season. There was an area of St Helier called Mount Bingham where all the courting couples would go for a snog in the long grass. We would go there at least once a week and snog but she never let me have my wicked way with her.

The Brett sisters left the island before we did but she did phone me at my digs in Jersey to ask me to keep in touch but I never did. However we did meet up some twenty years later when we both worked on the Bob Monkhouse Show... but that's a story for later.

Teddy, Bill and the Brett sisters.

At the end of that happy season Bill went back to Middlesbrough. But for me it was,
"Goodbye Jersey... hello London"

Chapter 5
Hello London

I arrived in London and made my way over to the Battersea area because Fred, one of the lads I met in Jersey, had given me his address saying,

"Me and Mam will put you up until you sort yourself out."

After knocking on the door of their home with my suitcase and you guessed it... guitar I still couldn't tune, they were true to their word and made me feel very welcome. It's not easy turning up at a town or city with no digs and no job – my first day in Blackpool and Manchester spring to mind – so I was very grateful to them both.

That night Fred took me to his local pub, "The Latchmere", to meet up with the lads I'd met in Jersey. It was a nice feeling to be amongst all those happy faces again. When I mentioned I was looking for digs someone said,

"What about Harry's place?"

"Who's Harry?" I asked.

"He owns the restaurant just across the road, he's got several rooms he lets off" explained Fred. "I'll nip over there now to see if he can put you up."

He returned with a big smile to say "Yes, Harry's got a small single room available which he's going to keep for you..."

But I had a sense there was something the lads weren't telling me.

And I was right because the next morning I turned up at the restaurant and met Harry only to find out he was outrageously gay and proud of it. As an ex West

End show dancer he was always ready to camp things up and show off his dancing skills in a very funny way. Remember this was 1960, a lot of gay men had not come out at that time and who could blame them because they were the butt of every comedians jokes even on the television.

However Harry soon realised which side of the fence I stood on and he turned out to be a funny man and a good landlord. The room I had was on the third floor, very tiny, but unlike the Salvation Army hostel, this one had a window. I recall opening the window at 2am one morning because loud singing and laughter had broken the silence and disturbed my sleep. What I saw was two dark skinned men either side of Harry carrying him home. I closed the window, covered my ears in the pillow and went back to sleep.

I woke the next morning, all was quiet and still, then I heard Sid coughing on one of his roll-up cigarettes... let me explain about Sid. He was chain smoking portly 65 year old friend of Harry's mother who was a very wealthy woman. She had bought the restaurant for Harry and had installed Sid in there to keep an eye on her only son... Incidentally I had never seen Sid without a unlit roll-up cigarette dangling out of his mouth. He was like a baby addicted to it's dummy. On a morning he would shave the right side of his face with the roll-up cigarette dangling in the left side of his mouth. He would move the cigarette to the other side of his mouth and then shave the left side of his face.

Anyway I entered the bathroom that morning to see a very concerned Sid. He looked at me long and hard and to my amazement, took the cigarette out of his mouth...

"You'll never guess what" he said with great concern pointing his finger in the direction of Harry's bedroom.

"What's wrong" I said.

"It's Harry" he replied... "he's only in bed there with two bloody spades" (spades being the terminology used at the time by some cockneys to describe a coloured immigrant.. hence the saying "as black as the ace of spades")

These are Sid's words, not mine. However I do recall my mother saying when I was a small boy,

"Look at your knees Our Teddy, they're as black as the ace of spades."

Needless to say Sid left the bathroom muttering to himself, "His mother will go spare if she finds out!"

Anyway back to the story.

Just up the road from Harry's place, the council were building several blocks of highrise flats. I got myself a job there as a joiners labourer. For digging the roads in Jersey I was paid £8 per week. For this job in London I was paid £12 per week.

"How good am I..."

Chapter 6
Finding Work

As a teenager I passed my driving test on a motor bike but I realised if I wanted to better myself in London, I would have to have a full driving license so I took ten lessons and passed my test first time.

"See, I told you I was good..."

I went for a job interview as a collector salesman. "Must have clean driving license" the advert had read. I went to an office in Clapham where I met the owner of the business, a man called Mr Pendrill.

He was a tall good looking man with the personality and all the trappings of a Hollywood film star. Everything about his dress was top quality from his hat down to his shoes. Add to that gold watch, gold cufflinks and rings. He explained in the interview that he had bought a new business and would need another salesman. He must have liked what he saw because he looked me straight in the eye and said,

"I'm willing to give you a try. Can you start Monday?"

"Yes," I said like a shot.

I was a bit nervous about telling the foreman on the building site I was leaving because the man had been good to me but all he said was,

"Don't worry. I knew you were meant for better things... So good luck to you son"

The first morning of my new job, Mr Pendrill called me into his office and handed me a set of keys.

"There's a small Austin van in the yard", he said " I want you to take my wife into the East End, she has to pick up some stock from the warehouse"

So I was sat in this little old van trying to get used to its long wobbly gear stick when the passenger door opened and this good looking elegant lady got in and said,

"Hello, you must be Teddy."

We shook hands and then I drove out of the yard into a side street with Mrs Pendrill happily chatting away unaware that I only had ten hours of driving experience.

We got to the main road and the traffic was very heavy. As I turned left to enter, my back wheel mounted the pavement and then came off with a mighty bump causing this tall elegant lady to bounce out of her seat and dislodge the nice hat she was wearing. The rest of the journey was a nightmare with me stalling the engine and other drivers blasting their horns at me. Consequently I was called into the office the next day and on learning I had just passed my test was told to take the spare van home with me and get some practice in.

Chapter 7
The Battersea Boys

That night Fred and I entered the Latchmere pub.
"Guess what?" said Fred "Teddy's only got himself a set of wheels..."

That remark was greeted with great excitement. Not many working class lads had transport in those days. So all my Battersea friends piled into the van and we went for a joyride.

"Let's go up the West End..." one of them shouted, so we did just that.

I remember it was dark and a bit foggy and at one point I turned into Trafalgar Square the wrong way much to the delight of all my friends in the van. Nevertheless a good night was had by all.

My old mate Bill came down to London and for the first couple of nights, had to crash out on the floor of my tiny room after declining the offer to sleep on the sofa in Harry's room, much to my amusement I must say.

However he soon got himself a bed-sit in the Baron's Court area of London. From then on our social life was good. I recall some months later going to the Richmond Castle Dance Hall where he later got the job as a band singer but on that particular night he met his future wife in the form of a nice looking dark haired girl called Margaret. Needless to say I didn't see much of Bill during the happy courting days with his future wife.

The job of a collector salesman was to call on your customers to collect a weekly payment on their account and try to sell them more of the firms goods. Once I was given the basic training I was very good at the job.

The problem for me was you had to carry a lot of stock; pots, pans and lots of ladies and gents fashion goods. Dresses, shirts, jumpers etc. You couldn't leave the stock in the van overnight which meant I had to carry it all up three flights of stairs into my tiny bedroom every night. I'm happy to say that problem was solved when I found a ground floor flat which came with a lockup garage.

I recall around that time buying a new Ford Cortina estate car. I fitted a rail in the back to hang all my fashion gear. One particular evening on my rounds in the Fulham area I had stopped at traffic lights and a car pulled alongside me with two large men inside. They both seemed to be taking a keen interest in the fashion goods and all the stock I was carrying.

I pulled away at the traffic lights and they slotted in behind me. I turned down a side street to make a call on a customer, they were still behind me. It was dark so I did a few more twists and turns and they were still following me. I was now very concerned about the stock, the firms takings for that day plus my own personal safety. I knew that the local police station was situated in a cul-de-sac a short distance away. I drove in that direction and they were still behind me. I stopped my car right outside the police station and locked myself in the car.

The two men were now out of their car and were banging on my window shouting at me to get out of my car... But I was having none of it, I put my hand on the horn and kept blasting away until I finally saw a uniformed police officer come out of the station and approach my car.

To my amazement the two villains did not turn and run because they turned out to be plain clothes police officers who thought I might have been a villain myself. When they checked out my credentials we all saw the funny side of the situation.

However I do recall one sad day around that time. I got home to my tiny flat and there was a telegram waiting for me. It was from my sister. I sat down on the bed and it just read:

"Sorry Teddy, our Dad died today, love Sheila"

I sat there on the bed and for some reason I couldn't cry but for the first time in my life I felt very sad and lonely. I never really knew the man but I recall as a small boy sitting on his knee and him singing to me the Al Jolson song "Little Pal". The opening lines to the song were:

"Daddy didn't have an easy time so what I couldn't be Little Pal, I want you to be Little Pal"

The telegram fell to the floor and I started to cry.
Years later I wrote a poem about that situation. It's called "Through the eyes of a Child."

"Through the Eyes of a Child"

> You died too early my father strong and left me all alone.
> I was angry with you then angry with God
> I thought that he should have known
> I go to my bed, no stories are read
> No strong hand any more just to hold
> There's no gentle nudge to open my eyes
> No warm kiss on the cheek no more smile
> These new people around are strange to my sound
> Some weak, some strong, they all try
> But they can't hold me as warm or guide me through storms
> Nor paint bright the inside of my mind

> With the passing of time, I'll grow strong
> in my mind
> And someday have children to care
> When they go to their beds, I'll remember
> the stories you read
> And that kiss on the cheek will be theirs

It was all very ironic really because a few months earlier I had gone to the parish priest in Middlesbrough to enquire how much it would cost to send my mother on a trip the church was running to the Holy Shrine Lourdes in France, something my mother had dreamed about all her life.

On learning the cost, I went to the post office and gave the money to the priest as payment for my mother go on the trip to Lourdes.

"That's a very nice gesture" the priest said. "You should be proud of yourself my son"

I was... and I still am because my mother had two sisters, both staunch Catholics with big families. On hearing about my gesture both families decided to send their mothers on the same trip. On hearing all this and knowing about my father's poor health, the parish priest decided my dad should go too and the church would pay the cost.

Everyone concerned was happy and excited about the whole situation but sadly my father died just a few weeks before the trip took place. However the sisters did go and never stopped talking about it for years. All this was instigated by little Teddy Lee! Something I'm still proud of to this day.

Chapter 8
The Dancing Times

The fact that I now had my own transport certainly enhanced my social life as I could call into the many pubs that had live music. Like down the Old Kent Road where I would get up and sing in the famous boxing pub "The Thomas Abeckitt", then move on to "The Rising Sun" and finish up in the "London Arms" before driving to the Lyceum Dancehall to finish the night off.

My other routine was to sing in a music pub in the Fulham Palace Road then drive on to the Hammersmith Palais.

Teddy singing in a pub.

I do recall one such night. I had driven past the Hammersmith Palais looking for somewhere to park and I noticed this bright neon sign saying "The

Garyhorn Club". I thought to myself... a nightclub! Great! I'll have some of that. I paid my entrance fee and the band were on their break but the place was packed and buzzing. I thought I'm sure to pull tonight.

I fought my way to the bar and bought myself a drink and waited with some excitement for the band to start up again, thinking the band leader would announce a quickstep or a foxtrot but no it was "Please take your partners for the Siege of Venus..." A loud caliegh band struck up and the floor was invaded with mad Irish couples stamping and jumping around like lunatics. I thought "Oh no, this is not a nightclub... it's a bloody Irish club". Needless to say I left thinking the only thing I'll pull in this mad house is a ligament!

I do remember one momentous night at the Hammersmith Palais. It started off bad and finished up good. Bad in the fact that I was dancing to a ladies and gentlemen's excuse me slow foxtrot. That meant a man could tap another man on the shoulder and say "Excuse me please". The man would leave allowing you to dance with his partner and the girls were at liberty to do the same.

This particular night my partner was excused. At first I was flattered, the lights were low and my new partner was tall and had long red hair. We danced around for a while and then I sensed something was wrong. The voice was deep and husky, the hands weren't soft like most girls hands are. Then it dawned on me. I thought,

"Oh shit, I'm dancing with a transvestite"

Fortunately the music stopped and I quickly walked away. I expressed my suspicions to one of the bouncers on the door. He said

" Is she tall with long red hair"

"Yes" I said.

He replied "That sounds like Davina. Her real name's David. We've barred her several times but she keeps sneaking back in. We do our best Sir but it's not easy with a place as big and popular as this"

That was the bad part of the evening.

The good part was the next girl I danced with turned out to be my future wife, Patricia who gave me a beautiful daughter and a handsome son and we all shared some great times together.

Chapter 9
Decision Time

It was round about this time that I decided to try and form myself a comedy act. So I wrote some gags and entered as many local pub talent shows as I could. I was very nervous at first but eventually started to relax and enjoy the experience. I moved on to shop windows. This is where the agents would attend and acts would audition in the hope of getting more work.

I met one agent who started to give me jobs in all the town halls and community centres around London entertaining our senior citizens. These shows would take place mainly on afternoons and were always an easy audience to perform to, unlike the pubs and clubs I was doing on a night time, which were just the opposite.

But I survived and it became very lucrative. That and my day job as a salesman meant "Little Teddy Lee" was doing alright for himself.

Chapter 10
Holiday Time

My wife and I had become very good friends with my old mate Bill and his wife Margaret. They had bought a villa on the beautiful island of Menorca and we decided to do the same. Both families shared some great times together.

I recall we bought a plot of land and told the builder what type of villa we would like. This was all a far cry from the tiny back street terraced house I was born into which had an outside toilet, no bathroom, two small bedrooms and no electricity. All this had to be shared with my mum, dad, three brothers and three sisters. So I was quite pleased and proud when at different times they all enjoyed my villa in Spain.

Especially my mother, who had never known what a holiday was like until then. I recall one happy moment, it was a very hot day and we were on the beach. Mum had left her swimming costume back at the villa and being a non-swimmer she decided to go into the water in her knickers and bra just to cool off. At one point she lost her balance and went under. She swallowed some sea water and started to splutter and panic and in the process lost her false teeth. Add to that, in getting wet her knickers and bra had become transparent so for the first time in my adult life I saw my mothers boobs. I started to guide her back towards the crowded beach and it did not help when my young son Paul drew peoples attention to my mothers plight by shouting,

"Nanna, we can see right through your knickers..."

Remember this was a woman of seventy five who had given birth to nine children... **so a page three girl she was not!**

So I went back into the sea with my snorkel gear and found her false teeth. I then took them all to the beach bar where we had a nice drink and bloody good laugh.

Nanna, Kim and Paul.

Chapter 11
Hen Nights

But to get back to the wannabe stuff! I saw an advert in "The Stage" newspaper. It read Singers wanted for the musical "Half a Sixpence". I went along to the auditions in a West End theatre. I took the sheet music to Frank Sinatra's "The French Foreign Legion". I put it in front of the pianist and started to sing out into the darkness of the theatre. Needless to say I was interrupted by a voice calling out,

" I'm sorry but that's not what we're looking for... Next please"

How daft can a wannabe get?

I was doing lots of pubs and clubs and around this time hen nights were very popular. The all female audience seemed to suit my style, whereas stag nights with an all male audience, were just the opposite. I wasn't blue enough and couldn't bring myself to swear on stage consequently I was compering lots of hen nights.

I've always enjoyed women's company so to be on stage and see your female audience laughing and enjoying themselves was a great feeling for me. On a hen night show you would get a compere, two drag acts and a male singer.

One particular drag act called Ron Ellis was popular and a very funny man. I worked with him a lot over the coming months. There was also a double drag act at the time doing comedy and mime. They had this weird guy who liked to hang around with them and act as their unpaid roadie. At one point in their act, he would run on the stage dressed in a big gorilla suit while they took the mickey out of him. Why would a normal man want to do that? It turned out he wasn't normal at all. Some months later the headline in the Daily Mirror was "Gorilla man strangles Drag Act in his bed" The drag act turned out to be the very talented Ron Ellis. We won't miss the gorilla man but there is a shortage of very funny men in this world.

Staying on the subject of hen nights, I did several on that famous ship HMS Belfast which is permanently moored in London on the river Thames.

On one particular night after the show, a speedboat came from a boat further down the river to pick up two drag acts and take them to a party. They invited me to come along but because I was married with two young children at the time, I had to say no. Which was a pity because the party was being hosted by Elton John on a boat he owned at the time. Looking back it would have been nice to say I met the very talented Mr Elton John.

But that was not to be... push on Teddy.

Chapter 12
My time in Jail

I've been in prison twice in my life, the first time it was in Wandsworth and I was there to entertain the inmates but I was being put off because the prison vicar was sat in the front row. He must have realized he was spoiling things because he left and I immediately changed tack and said,

"Hands up all the gays in this prison"

Someone shouted "there's only one and he's just left"

From then on everything was fine and my act went down very well.

My second visit to prison was different because it was the famous Holloway women's prison. You had two tiers of cells each side of the hallway with a wide space in between where benches had been put for the inmates to sit. A small stage had been put in place at one end with a curtained off area which was to be our dressing room.

There were stone floors with iron bars and steel doors all around. The whole place was cold and dour except for the women sat on those benches... they were a captivated audience and great!

A uniformed prison officer stood on the stage and announced:

"Right ladies, let's get the show started with your compere Mr Teddy Lee..."

I emerged from behind the curtain all suited and booted and the place just erupted and I hadn't even said a word. The warmth and the laughter that came from those women that night turned that big cold prison into a warm and cosy room. And a good time was had by all...

Chapter 13
Audition Time

It was around this time that I did an audition for Hughie Green's "Opportunity Knocks". I found him to be a kind and considerate man. He took the trouble to explain that gags about TV adverts were not suitable for the BBC and encouraged me to come back again.

But two weeks later I went to the Victoria Palace Theatre and auditioned for ITV's "New Faces". This time I got a letter back saying I had passed and they would write to me with a date to go on the show. When this did not happen I contacted them by phone and was told the producer of the show had left and the new producer was not prepared to put any artist on that he had not personally auditioned himself. They eventually let me talk to the new producer and it was agreed that if I was prepared to go to Birmingham to do a private audition in his office, he would reconsider.

So the next day I drove to Birmingham, did my three minute routine with just him sat at his desk. He liked what he saw, took a list out of his desk drawer and gave me a date there and then. I got back in my car and drove all the way back to Walton on Thames. How about that for a dedicated wannabe?

In the late sixties I had joined the Variety Artist Union. The annual fee was 5 shillings in old money, about 25p in today's currency. Some years later they amalgamated with Equity Union and the fee was increased dramatically so I decided to drop out. Unbeknown to me there was a ruling with Equity that if a member had no work, he could lodge his equity card which meant he could be re-instated at any time in the future, when work was available.

Roll the clock forward from the late sixties to 1975, I was sat at home with a letter from ITV stating that no-one could appear on "New Faces" show unless they were Equity members. For all the other contestants, that was just a formality and they were automatically accepted but for Little Teddy Lee who had not lodged his card all those years earlier, I had to pay up all the back fees. I was paid £112 for appearing on "New Faces" and a large amount of that went to Equity! How unlucky can a wannbe get?

"New Faces" was recorded on a Wednesday and shown on TV the following Saturday night and they would always get 12 million viewers because at that time there was only three stations to choose from, BBC1, BBC2 plus ITV.

So one day in May back in 1975, Little Teddy Lee drove up to Birmingham once again to seek his fame and fortune on the television... I think not!

Let me explain. I checked in at the Studios on time at 10am and was told to wait in the canteen till they called me on the tannoy system. All the other artistes on the show had been called the day before because they had to rehearse with the orchestra, whereas I didn't. Consequently they were all chatting happily away to each other while I sat on my own like... "Little Billy No Mates".

After sitting there for two hours a voice over the tannoy said,

"Will Teddy Lee come to Studio one please."

I thought, good, a chance for me to rehearse my three minute routine only to be told by the floor manager that all they wanted from me was a voice level for the sound engineer. After I'd said about there words, the floor manager said,

"That's fine Teddy, we've got what we want so you can go back to the canteen and we'll call you later for a full dress rehearsal"

Just before that, the floor manager spoke to all the artistes saying it's very expensive to stop the show so if any of you make a mistake, just keep going because the cameras will be filming you and it will stay in the show. In other words treat it like you're doing a pub or a club and just keep going.

Teddy on "New Faces".

For me the dress rehearsal went OK, I was dressed in my velvet jacket and my blue frilly shirt. The judging panellists came in and they consisted of Arthur Askey, Mickey Most and a female showbiz columnist from one of the daily newspapers. They watched the rehearsal and made notes to help them form comments for the live show. The only one missing was the hatchet man himself – Tony Hatch. He liked to watch the live show and speak off the top of his head. You had to admire the man for that as he was the original Mr Nasty and all the other Mr Nasty's that followed were just replicas.

Anyway here's the best bit! After the dress rehearsal with just two hours to go before the live show, the powers that be decided that some of my gags were not suitable and had to be changed. I complained bitterly and pointed out it was the same routine I had done three weeks ago so why was I not told then? But they were having none of it... Just when I was starting to relax a bit they do this to me...

Anyway, in their wisdom, they gave me a dressing room to myself so I could rehearse my new stuff. I remember taking off my jacket and shoes because the room was so warm. I was rehearsing in front of this long mirror and at one point I heard over the tannoy,

"Will Johnny Patrick and the orchestra go to Studio one please"

When they took all the artists from the main dressing room to the studio to start filming the show, they automatically thought everyone was there... but I wasn't.

Unbeknown to me the show had started and I was the next act on and everything was panic stations backstage.

Back in my dressing room, over the tannoy I heard,

"Will Teddy Lee go to Studio one immediately, I repeat immediately."

I picked up my shoes, grabbed my jacket and ran to Studio One. On entering I was met by a very irate floor manager. His first words were,

"You bastard, where have you been?"

My first thoughts were "Sod you mate... I'm going home."

But I could hear the compere's voice saying,

"And the next act comes from the North East..."

So I thought "No Teddy, you've got to do this...." so I put on my velvet jacket, slipped into my shoes and walked bravely through the curtain into the bright lights of Studio One... and the rest is just a blur in my memory...

I can't remember doing any of my routine and from my position on the podium you could not hear what the panel were saying about your act. But at the end of it all I heard the compere say,

"And we see Teddy breathe a sigh of relief as he steps down from the podium..."

How bloody right he was.

Chapter 14
The Commercial

The good thing that came out of the "New Faces" experience was my Equity card because that enabled me to try and get some TV work.

In my ignorance I started calling at the offices of casting directors, leaving photos of myself, something I learned later you just do not do that. Because that is the job of your agent and I didn't have one. I recall knocking on the door of a very smart household in a posh area of Chelsea. A nice lady answered the door and I started to explain that I was looking for some TV work. I could see she was quite amused by my naiveté and invited me and my baby face in. She asked some questions and then I gave her some photos and details about myself and left.

The lady's name I think was Jessica Martin. Two days later she phoned me saying...

"Teddy, I'd like you to go for a casting tomorrow. Are you available?"

"Yes" I said thinking to myself, "What's a casting..."

Anyway I turned up at an office in Soho and waited in reception along with several actors who were up for the same part. I learnt from their conversation that they were all established actors and the part we were auditioning for was for the central character in a Shell commercial. The Director was Franc Roddam, a very well known film and television director. The film "Quadrafenia", TV's "Boys from the Blackstuff" and "Auf Viedersen Pet" were all credited to him.
It didn't help when the receptionist called out,

"Can Mr Roddam take a phone call from Glen Ford in Hollywood..."

Glen Ford was a big big Hollywood film star at the time...

I thought "Shit Teddy Lee, you're out of your depth this time"

I was the last one to go in for my audition. Franc Roddam was behind a long bench like table. There was a chair the other side for me. I was surprised by how young he looked. His first words were,

"You look a bit nervous Teddy.. what's wrong?"

I thought "Sod it... tell the man the truth..."

"I've never done anything like this before. I just do cabaret in the clubs and pubs."

His next question was,

"Where's that accent from?"

"Middlesbrough" I replied.

He leaned across the table, looked me in the eye and said,

"Snap!"

He was also from the Boro. His next question was,

"What job did you do there?"

My reply was "The last job was in Smiths Dock Shipyards"

He leaned forward and said,

"Snap!" again.

I got the impression he was enjoying our conversation. His next request was,

"Teddy, I want you to walk to the end of the room, touch the wall, turn round and come back and sit down again

That, I gather, was for him to see how I moved. We spoke a while longer. We stood up and shook hands and then I left.

Later that day I got a call from Jessica Martin to say I had got the job. It was to be a three day shoot at £200 per day plus repeat fees. That was a lot of money back in those days... She asked for details of my agent and laughed when I told her I didn't have one. She advised me to write to the advertising company Ogilvy, Benson and Mather and inform them I was self managed so they could send all the money and repeat fees direct to me.

The commercial was shown on all the TV stations in the UK so as I result I was to get repeat fees from all of them which proved to be very lucrative... Yippee!

What a lucky wannabe am I.

The gist of the commercial was me as a Shell lorry driver delivering central heating oil to a home and school and farm. There was an animated little Shell character moving about from time to time in front of the screen action with a musical jingle, I think, being sung by none other than Bing Crosby himself. That must have cost them a packet!

The first day's filming seemed to go OK. We were called at 8am and the location was out in the countryside in Buckinghamshire. The second day's call was at 7am. The reason for that (unbeknown to me) was they hadn't got the early morning shot they wanted and were hoping to get it the next day. So on that second morning, I turned off the M4 at the wrong exit and got lost for a while. As a result I was very late.

I was greeted on location by a very concerned wardrobe lady who ushered me into my boilersuit uniform and explained they were trying to film the early morning scene without me. I have since learnt the cardinal sin in the film business:

That if you are an important cog in the wheel you must... never be late.

I went onto the set and saw the producer talking to several suited big wigs from the Shell Oil company. I went over and tried to apologize. They never said a word. Their frozen faces just glared at me till I mumbled sorry again and turned away. The comment from the Director Franc Roddam was,

"Let's put this behind us Teddy and get on with this shoot".

Some days later he took the trouble to phone me and say everyone was very pleased with the end result and that a very good friend who's opinion he valued had said the choice of me as the central character was very good casting.

So I would just like to say thanks to Franc Roddam for being a very good director and a very nice human being.

Chapter 15
The Wine Bar

Like a lot of entertainers when they are a bit fed up or disillusioned with show business, their thoughts turn to owning their own pub and I was at that stage in my life. Coming home in the early hours, drinking a few whiskeys to help you unwind... is not a good way of life.

Anyway, just a walking distance from where I was living in Walton on Thames, a new shopping centre was being built. I took an option out on one of the vacant units and got a full liquor license from the local magistrates, despite strong opposition from the local publicans. I sold my villa in Spain to help me fund the project and with the help of my younger brother Bill, who was an excellent carpenter, turned that empty shell of a shop unit into a posh upmarket wine bar called... "Tippler's Wine Bar"

One amusing thing that happened was the three magistrates who granted my license for the wine bar paid a visit shortly after we opened. They bought and paid for a drink and then had a meal. When they left my daughter Kim informed me they hadn't paid their bill for the food. I thought it was funny that I had to chase these three pillars of the community and tell them in street that they had not paid their bill.

I jokingly said...

"Do you want to pay the bill... or should I call the police?"

They did not see the funny side of my remark... however they did pay up.

Chapter 16
Sleeping with the Devil

Unfortunately one of the local publicans who opposed my license was stirring his customers up and sending them over to my wine bar to cause trouble.

This was causing great problems for me especially at the weekend when the bar was popular and very busy.

One night, unbeknown to me this big guy came in to settle an old score and a fight broke out. By the time the police arrived the troublemakers had gone and when I described the big guy to the police sergeant.

He said "That sounds like Mick Kelly, he drinks in the local social club up the road and he used to be a bouncer at one of the nightclubs in town." I went into the social club the following night and Mick Kelly was sat at a table drinking with his two brothers.

My first impression was if I was directing a movie and wanted three big scary villains, they were there right in front of me.

Anyway, I walked over to the table and told Mick Kelly he was barred from my wine bar for causing trouble. To my surprise he dropped his head and sheepishly apologised. What I later learnt about Mick Kelly was if you challenged him mentally he was shy and awkward but if you challenged him physically he was fearless and in his element.

So one week later, who should I find enjoying a drink in my crowded bar... Mr Mick Kelly!

I walked over and looked up at him and said,

"I thought I told you not to come in here again."

His reply was,

"I like it here, the music's good and there's always nice looking girls in here."

It was then that I had a brainwave... and said,

"I hear you used to be a bouncer in one of the nightclubs in town?"

His reply was "Yes."

So I explained the problem I was having with some of the local lads so I then offered him the job as doorman at the weekend on a trial period and agreed to pay him £10 per night and we shook hands on that arrangement.

So there I was getting into bed with the devil!

And it worked like a dream. Because no one wanted to cross swords with Mick Kelly because if they did they would have to contend with the rest of the Kelly family... so for me that was the problem solved! All this free of charge because the amount Mick Kelly and his brothers spent over the bar more than covered his ten pound in wages... see I'm not stupid all the time!

Chapter 17
Grab a Granny Night

It was around this time that my marriage started to go wrong and eventually ended in divorce. Fortunately my daughter Kim and son Paul were young working adults and by that time had left the family home. Nevertheless it was still a sad time for all concerned. And it prompted me to write a song. These are some of the words from it,

Chorus
I won't make you cry anymore
You can't take the pain that's for sure
We both walked away
And sadly I say
I won't make you cry anymore

Verse
Whoever we meet in our future times
Can't travel the roads that we've left behind
They can't talk of daughter or son that you bore
Nor share memories that you and I store
And so I won't make you cry anymore

So, after twenty three years of marriage I was a single man again. A friend of mine called Phil who was also a single man suggested we go to a DSS disco night which was being held at a local hotel... DSS was short for Divorced, Single and Separated, also known as "Grab a granny night"!

Phil and I had not been to one of these nights before but he had been informed a lot of single girls also attended so we decided to give it a go. On entering the said venue all suited and booted, we found there was a nice mixture of old and young. We bought a couple of drinks and started to optimistically survey the possibilities. Then from the other side of the dancefloor we saw this elderly granny type lady waving at us as she walked across the empty dancefloor towards us. At this point Phil dropped his head in despair and said.

"Oh no... it's only my bloody Aunty Norah".

After being introduced to Phil's Aunty Norah, I excused myself and had a dance with a nice blond girl. Sometime later as I left the disco with my nice blond friend, I saw my mate Phil reluctantly jiving with his Aunty Norah.

"Well you win some... you lose some... Good night Phil".

Chapter 18
Meeting Kate

Some months later I was driving along by the river Thames with a friend of mine when he noticed a pub ahead of us and said,

"Lets have a drink in there."

So I quickly turned into the car park and we went in for a drink.

Little did I know but that decision would happily effect the rest of my life because I later met a tall good looking, well educated Australian girl called Kate and we've been partners, lovers and best friends for the last twenty three years. Kate has always inspired and encouraged me to write and has spent endless hours typing my scripts and songs and I will always be eternally grateful for that.

I think the best way to describe my feelings for Kate is in this poem I wrote about her some time ago. It goes like this...

> From the very first day that I met her
> There was never a moment of doubt
> That she was the only girl for me
> Till the light that is my life goes out
> And if there is life after this event
> And the spirits are friendly and nice
> I'll wait... and I'll wait for the spirit that's Kate
> And we'll kiss and move on through that life.

Thanks for everything Kate and I hope when you type these words you won't get embarrassed too much.

I must explain to the readers I'm poor at spelling, write very slowly and make lots of mistakes. Consequently I write everything with a pencil that has a rubber on the end. And all this time you thought Little Teddy Lee was a clever intellectual.... WRONG!

Incidentally the pub where I met Kate was called "The Bell" and the landlord was that well known wrestler Steve Viedor. Both Kate and I have some happy memories of the fine hospitality and friendship we shared with Steve and his lovely wife Jenny.

Chapter 19
The Bush Wedding

So let me tell you about one of my most memorable times. It wasn't at Shepperton or Pinewood studios or on any big film set. It was at a station, not a railway station, but a sheep station in outback Australia.

Everything Kate and I did seemed to be a big adventure at the time but for me this was top of the list. It was the outback wedding of Kate's sister Helen. She was getting married to her boyfriend Waldo.

We landed at Sydney airport and hired a big Ford car, top of the range with all the latest extras including cruise control. Which was great when you are driving on those long straight endless roads that take you to the outback.

We had booked to stay at the Sydney Hilton hotel for the first night. I remember driving up to the big impressive hotel entrance. I got out of my big car and handed the keys to the impressively dressed concierge who had it driven to the car park. This made me feel like James Bond 007 but looking more like Little Teddy Lee, 003 and a half.

So the next day we drove off the long straight road onto the dirt track that would eventually bring us to Kate's parent's sheep station. You could not drive fast on those bumpy old tracks which was just as well as several times I had to slow down to let kangaroos pass. You don't see anything like that in the Northeast of England.

On arriving at the farm, I felt I was a privileged guest as we were allocated the bedroom with the brand new air conditioning unit. And boy did I need it!

Anyway the first morning they put up this huge marquee which Billy Smart's circus would have been proud of.

Kate's family in the aftermath of the bush wedding - with dogs.

The following day was the day of the wedding. The first to arrive were all the waitresses. Then the guest started to arrive, around 200 of them, in their four wheel drives. When I first walked into the marquee just before the ceremony was due to take place, I was most impressed. The floor was all carpeted and nice table and chairs all in place. There was an alter at one side and a busy bar at the other with 200 happy Australians enjoying themselves. The whole marquee was bursting with a brilliant atmosphere.

The priest entered dressed immaculately in the traditional way. MGM Studios could not have created a better scene. The priest called for attention and asked for the bar to be closed. The whole marquee became very quiet. The groom and the best man were in place immaculate in their tuxedos. The beautiful bride entered and the whole ceremony was conducted to perfection with Little Teddy Lee soaking up all the action of this unique occasion feeling proud and privileged to be part of it.

It was a great experience to visit Kate's family and be part of their every day working lives. I recall one of the early days of my first visit, Kate's three brothers, all a lot taller than me I might add, came into the kitchen and said,

"We're going out on the truck to shoot a roo",

Would I like to come with them?

I didn't know what the hell they meant, but I said yes!

So there was I sat on the back of this small open truck with Kate's three brothers. One of them was carrying a telescopic rifle. So unbeknown to me, we were driving out into the bush looking for a kangaroo to shoot... why would they want to do that?

Because there were 12 working sheep dogs on the farm that had to be fed and occasionally they liked some fresh meat. So this was one way of doing it...

"Can you fire a rifle" said Joe, the elder of the brothers.

"I've only fired an air rifle at the local fair" I replied.

This brought a smile from the brothers. So they stopped the truck and we all got out. They placed an empty beer bottle on a rock some twenty or so metres away and the telescopic rifle was handed to me.

How many times have we seen this in those Hollywood cowboy movies I thought to myself. Anyway I did as I was instructed and focused the telescopic lens on the neck of the bottle and moved slowly down to the wider part and gently squeezed the trigger. And bingo... the bottle shattered into tiny pieces.

So, some twenty minutes later they stopped the truck again. Because they had spotted... a dogs dinner for 12 in the form of a kangaroo. It was feeding peacefully under the tree some five hundred metres away. It was then that I heard those dreaded words as Joe whispered,

"Quick give the rifle to Teddy."

They all then stepped back a few paces so I was stood alone just me, the telescopic rifle and the kangaroo.

"Go on take aim!" I heard them whisper. So I looked through the telescopic lens and focused on the kangaroo's head as it was happily nibbling the leaves of the tree. So you decide if this was a happy ending or not.

Because I squeezed the trigger, the bullet missed the kangaroo, hit the tree and the dogs dinner for 12 skipped happily away into the bush, never to be seen again...

Needless to say I still vividly remember that day, some twenty years on.

Chapter 20
Handcuffed

There is something very undignified about being handcuffed especially with your hands behind your back. This happened to me on an episode of "The Bill". The handcuffs and the key is the responsibility of the man who works in the property department... he is known as the props man. So, at the end of this long and complicated scene, I breathed a sigh of relief and informed the Director that I was bursting for a pee. He shouted out,

"Props... unlock Teddy please!"

When there was no response he shouted out again only to be told that Dennis the props man who had the keys to unlock me had gone back to the studios in the van to pick up some lighting equipment and had taken the keys with him.

The Director stood scratching his head and said,

"Oh shit Teddy, I'm sorry about this... could one of the lads take you to the toilet?"

Needless to say I shook my head vigorously at this suggestion. He then pointed to Sue, a nice looking girl from the make-up department but she was having none of it... so with my arms handcuffed behind my back, I had to cross my legs tightly till Dennis the props man returned.

Later that day Dennis the props man was setting up for a fight scene and I noticed he had a box full of those fake bottles that when you hit someone over the head, they shatter into small pieces. My immediate thought was I could have some fun with them in my local pub. I asked Dennis if I could take a couple, his reply was,

"Teddy, after today's cock up with your handcuffs, that's the least I can do for you."

So a few nights later, Kate and I were going to a fancy dress party at the Manor Bar in Shepperton High Street. So with the owners' permission, a local businessman called John Lee, I placed the fake bottles behind the bar close to the till so at the height of the evening and the bar packed with happy drinkers, the plan was for me to go behind the bar and accuse Darrell, the barman, of short changing me.

So everything was in place, I was stood at the end of the bar having a drink with Kate and my daughter Kim. Unbeknown to me, stood next to Kim, was a friend of John Lee's who was also a professional cagefighter. I entered the bar and start shouting my accusations at Darrell. Only a few people were in on the joke, everyone else in the bar thought it was for real... including John's friend the cagefighter.

So I whacked the bottle over Darrell's head and it shattered and Darrell fell to the floor. Some of the drinkers screamed out in horror. Mr Pedders, the bar manager tried to intervene so I whacked him over the head with the other fake bottle and he went down.

But the best fight of the night was between my daughter Kim and the cagefighter who thinking everything was for real, wanted to get behind the bar and sort me out. I'm happy to say my daughter won that argument.

"Phew, thanks Kim!"

I was offered some work as a driver by an old friend of mine called Paul. He worked for a company that supplied all the cars and police vehicles to "The Bill". It turned out to be regular work and a pleasant job because of all the nice people there.

About that time my son Paul owned a pub restaurant and every year we used to raise money for the Charity

"Children in Need". I got permission from the powers that be to raise money at "The Bill". We held a raffle and I wrote some short comedy sketches which all the cast members were happy to appear in.

Three people who stand out in my memory is the delightful Lisa Maxwell who played a Detective Inspector, Graham Cole as Tony Stamp and Alex Wilkinshaw as Smithy. They made themselves available to make short films and show them in my son's pub.

There are several incidents that I look back on and smile. One was when we arrived at a river location for the crew to set up their cameras. Some of the lads were keen fisherman and were annoyed and angry when they saw some East European men fishing out of season. They tried to explain and to get them to stop but they kept saying,

"No understand,"

They carried on fishing much to the annoyance of the crew. But we had the last laugh when a few minutes later, the uniformed Tony Stamp drove up in his police car ready to start filming. The East Europeans thought he was for real and quickly packed up their fishing rods and scarpered.

"Nice one Tony Stamp!"

Needless to say the rest of the day's filming went quite well.

Chapter 21
Meeting The Stars

Because I was an equity member again, I was allowed to do film work. My first job was with David Jason on a TV show called "A Sharp intake of Breath". In one scene he was being chased by some mad woman who wanted to whack him over the head with her umbrella.

I was the same height, build and hair colour as David, so they chose me to be his double. The scene was David Jason runs out of a shopping centre wearing a red jumper and dark grey slacks and disappears into the crowd. The mad woman runs out, looks around and gets a back view of me in a phone box wearing a red jumper and dark grey slacks. She opens the door and is just about to whack me when I turn round and she realizes it's a case of mistaken identity.

Incidentally during a break in filming I recall David Jason doing a very good impression of Humphrey Bogart... is there no end to that man's talent?

Some months later I got a phone call from the Production team of "Only Fools and Horses". It was explained to me they wanted a shot of Delboy and Rodney arriving at Kennedy airport in New York but for some reason David Jason was not available. The thinking was they would get a shot in this country of the plane's door opening. Delboy and Rodney would step out, look around and start to walk down the steps. They would then get a back view shot of me dressed in Delboy's clothes walking down the steps and across the tarmac at Kennedy airport with a big sign saying "Welcome to Kennedy airport".

The production company were prepared to fly me out with the character Rodney to Kennedy airport to get the back shot required and then fly us straight back again. But when I was given the date they wanted to do it, I was on holiday and not available.

Some years later they were considering me to be David Jason's stand in on "A Touch of Frost" but when they found out how old I was, they decided to go for someone younger.

I recall doing two days extra work on a film called "Funny Bones". Two of the stars were Jerry Lewis, the American comedian and the bad boy himself Oliver Reed.

The scene was a very posh garden party. I was stood close by Oliver Reed for most of the day. He looked smart, fit, well-behaved and was word perfect all day. I thought his bad boy image was all exaggerated by the press.

But the next day's shoot was at a small airport in Surrey. There was a private aeroplane on the runway with a red carpet leading up to a small stage. Stood in front of the microphone was the mayor and mayoress of Blackpool. They were there to greet the famous American comedian Jerry Lewis.

At this point Oliver Reed staggered on to the set drinking out of a plastic cup, clearly very drunk. He would walk up to any one of the extras he thought was looking at him and stick his big fist under their nose. The crew managed to get him to sit down off set and out of view of the cameras.

The scene was Jerry Lewis, the American celebrity was to get off the plane, walk down the red carpet with all the extras applauding him. He was to step on to the stage to be greeted by the mayor and mayoress of Blackpool. The first take was spoilt by Oliver Reed shouting in the background. On the second take he dived on to the stage and rugby tackled the mayor and mayoress and brought them to the floor along with the mike stand.

The next thing a car turned up with three big security guards who bundled Oliver Reed into the car and drove him away, never to be seen again on that picture! I later read in the press that Joanna Lumley was supposedly paid £30,000 for a scene she was to do that day with Oliver Reed but she was never in the picture... I wonder why?

Some years later while filming on the island of Malta, a man was found dead in a bar. The film was "Gladiator"... the dead man was... Oliver Reed. How very sad!

I recall getting a day's work as a photographer on the Spice Girls film. They were at the height of their fame and my thoughts on seeing them was how tiny they all were, that is with the exception of Scary Spice who I got the opportunity to talk to. Why they call her scary I'll never know, she came across as a nice friendly girl from Leeds.

In the picture they were being interviewed by Jonathan Ross outside the Royal Albert Hall. I had written a song at the time which I thought would have suited the Spice Girls and I had a copy on a cassette in my pocket in the hope of getting one of them interested. My best opportunity was while I was talking to Scary Spice but looking at the costume she was wearing which was tight fitting and had no pockets, I thought if I gave her my cassette, where would she put it? I thought my best chance would be in the lunch break but that was not to be because the security was very strict and no one could get anywhere near them. So take your cassette home with you and dream on my son...

I was compering a show one night with Bob Monkhouse at the top of the bill. At the end of the night he asked for one of my cards explaining that my act did not clash with anything he did and could possibly use me as a compere in the future which he did, on several occasions. He also gave me a small part on a TV show he was doing at the time.

We did a sketch where we had a custard pie fight. Later Bob and I were sat in make up being cleaned up when this gay man came in and said,

"Teddy... were you in Jersey in 1959!"

After Bob Monkhouse had given me one of his cheeky – who's been a naughty boy then – looks, I said to the man,

"Yes. Why?"

His reply was, "My friend in Wardrobe, she's been looking at the monitor and she thinks she knows you.."

It turned out to be my friend from the Brett sisters all those years earlier. We went for a drink after the show and had a good old chat about our times in Jersey then both went our separate ways.

I was booked to compere another show with Bob Monkhouse at a very large pub venue in Essex. Bob had to pull out at the last moment and was replaced by the Irish tenor Joseph Lock. I had worked the venue before; the audience consisted mainly of young men all standing with drinks. You also had a long noisy bar to contend with. Everyone there had paid to see Bob Monkhouse so I feared for the reception an Irish tenor might get. He was well known to the older generation but most of this audience had never heard of him.

My fears were right because he struggled all through his act and he finished on a song called "Goodbye". He asked the audience to join in which they did with great gusto but their version of "Goodbye" had an F at the front of it and an OFF at the end. But he finished the song, took a bow and walked off with great dignity.

I later apologised to Joseph Lock for the crowd's behaviour. He gave me a big Irish smile and said,

"If you can't handle failure son, you'll never handle success."

Yes all the good old pros know how to die a death with great dignity. So rest in peace Mr Joseph Lock.

Chapter 22
Welcome to Wales

The Joseph Lock treatment reminded me of the first time I died a death on stage. It was a working mans club in Wales. A colleague had already warned me about this club saying,

"If you can't sing like Harry Secombe, don't do it."

I should have taken his advice because my spot in the first half, I struggled big time and my spot in the second half of the show was even worse because they started to close the curtains before I was finished. I defiantly held back the curtains, finished what I had to say, bowed to the audience and walked off.

It's hard when something like that happens especially to a young performer learning his trade. So I was feeling very despondent as I packed my gear into the car on this very dark night in this remote part of Wales.

Imagine the shock I got when I saw a pair of eyes just a few feet away staring at me through the bushes of this dark desolate car park. I backed away in fright and in the process dropped my car keys. While I was fumbling on the floor looking for them, still terrified of those staring eyes, there was a movement in the bushes and the eyes started to move towards me. Then out of the bushes stepped this big fat sheep, it gave a couple of bleats and wandered off into the darkness of a nearby field.

That just about made my night complete. Goodbye Wales!

Some time later I spoke about it to that fine Irish comic Dave Allen when we shared a dressing room and a glass of whiskey together and he said,

"Don't worry about it Teddy... it's happened to me more than once. It's just part of the learning curve we all have to go through."

Chapter 23
Give that Dog a Bone

But to get back to the wannabe stuff... I had a big handsome Doberman dog called Butch. We often worked together. On this occasion it was back on the police program "The Bill". I was to be a security officer and Butch was to be my guard dog.

Some time previously I had taken Butch to the vets to be castrated. The surgery had a hard slippery floor. Consequently any time after that when Butch came into contact with a hard slippery floor, he immediately thought he was going to have his balls cut off again and he would crouch down like a scared rabbit and you would have to drag him across the slippery floor.

Anyway, there I was in reception dressed in my security guard uniform with Butch on a lead next to me. Then a girl approached and said,

"Teddy, the Director wants to see you and the dog and have a photograph taken."

So we followed the girl across the nice carpeted area of reception to a set of swing doors. The girl held the swing doors open. I could see the Director sat at a table on the other side of this large room which you guessed it... had a hard slippery floor. I entered followed by Butch but as soon as he got the feel of the hard slippery floor, he crouched down and went into his scared rabbit routine. I had to start to drag him across the hard slippery floor. The other thing about Butch was that when he was really scared he had no control over his waterworks. Consequently when I finally got him to the Directors table, there was a long line of dog pee stretching all the way back to the swing doors.

The first thing the bewildered Director said was,

"Teddy, he's supposed to be a bloody guard dog"

I explained everything to the Director and he saw the funny side of it. We went outside onto solid ground and we got the photographs he wanted. And everything was fine.

Teddy and Butch

The other problem Butch had was because he was such a handsome dog, people were attracted and always wanted to stroke him. That was fine if you were a man but if you were a woman the first thing he wanted to do was stick his nose in between a woman's legs and have a good old sniff at her ladygarden. This was very embarrassing especially if the lady was wearing a dress. I recall one lady assistant director as Butch was doing his unmanly act, the embarrassed lady turned to her Director and said,

"He can probably smell my dog."

The Director's reply which brought a big laugh from all the crew was,

"You haven't got a bloody dog."

I had a day's work with Butch on a TV show called "As Time Goes By". The leading lady on this was none other than the very talented and much respected Dame Judi Dench who I understand happened to be a dog lover. My action on the show was to walk past with Butch as she was coming out of a shop. The Assistant Director thought it would be wise to forewarn Dame Judi that I would be walking past her with a large Doberman dog. She looked in our direction and I'm sorry to say she was wearing a nice soft flowing dress.

Her first words as she walked towards Butch were,

"Oh what a beautiful dog..."

Needless to say Butch must have realised he was in the presence of a very special lady because he just... sat there all regal like and offered Dame Judi his paw...Phew! Give that dog a bone.

Chapter 24
Writing Time

Around this time I was doing a lot of writing in the hope of something being accepted by the big TV companies. I spent several years sending scripts and sketches trying to break into that side of show business only to have everything sent back saying...

"Thanks but no thanks"

I recall having an idea for a situation comedy. I wrote the first 30 minute episode and sent it off to the BBC. To my surprise I had a reply saying they would be interested to see where future episodes would go. I slaved away for weeks and wrote two more episodes together with a song that would complement the show and with great expectations sent them off to the BBC.

After several weeks I got a reply saying,

"We thought long and hard about your scripts but in the end decided not to go with them..."

What was my situation comedy called?

EXTRAS!

Imagine how I felt when five years later Ricky Gervais wrote his version of "Extras". How unlucky can a wannabe get? Strangely enough I did a day's work on his show "The Office". Oh well, you win some, you lose some... But please God, let me win just once!

I still have that letter and those scripts to this day.

Chapter 25
The Jobs I Never Got

I auditioned for "Britain's Got Talent" at the impressive Xcel Centre in London. I performed one of my own songs which seemed to impress the lady because she let me finish the song, which is always a good sign, and then asked the camera man to keep filming as she asked me further questions about myself. I told her I had written a script about talent shows. I then gave her a synopsis of the script and left with the feeling that I had done well. But the powers that be thought differently because I heard no more from them. Maybe it was a mistake trying to flog one of my scripts to them... so another one bites the dust. Move on son.

I've been for lots of auditions in my time so let me tell you about one job I was glad I never got! It was a photographic job for a company called "Royals" that sold men's jeans. They were looking for a builder type of character who had a good bum cleavage. I was reassured by the agent that they only wanted a back shot of my bum and my face would not be shown.

I had to wear a very short tight T-shirt and a pair of the company's jeans. The photographer and his assistant were both gay and very fussy. The photographer said,

"Teddy, turn round and face the wall. Put your arms out in front of you. Spread your legs wide, now lean forward and let your hands support your body just like the police do when they are searching a suspected criminal".

The photographer then turned to his assistant and said,

"What do you think Rodney?"

The reply came back,

"Hmmm... yes... but I think the line of his jeans needs to come down a little bit more so we can see more of his cleavage. Teddy love, we're just going to loosen your belt and pull your jeans down a bit more, is that alright...."

Well, I can tell you at this stage I was not a happy bunny. I've never had two gay men fussing round my backside before... I am happy to say!

So, after taking several shots the photographer said,

"Right Teddy, I want you to hold your body in that position but turn your head round as far as you can and look straight at the camera. So much for my agent saying your face won't be shown!

Anyway I did as I was told and on the way out I met Big Dave, a chubby lad who was also up for the part. I'm very happy to say that Big Dave got the part because some weeks later there was a massive billboard campaign all over the country with Big Dave's face and cleavage. The billboard read:

"If you want to show your bum cleavage, get yourself a pair of Royals the best jeans in town"

See, it's not all a bed of roses being a wannabe!

Chapter 26
Frankenstein

It was always nice to get work at Shepperton Studios because Kate and I lived there and it meant I could nip home in my lunch break and take our dog Butch out.

So I was pleased when I got several days work on a film called "Frankenstein"... starring Robert de Niro, Kenneth Branagh (who was also the Director) and that well known actress Helena Bonham Carter.

On the first morning Wardrobe dressed me up as a poor village peasant in scruffy clothes and put a dirty old wig on my head. They sent me off to make-up where they painted my teeth yellow, then decided that a couple at the front should be painted black. Add to that several pox marks on my face and neck... not a pretty sight I can tell you... Consequently when I went home at lunch time to take my dog Butch out he didn't recognise me and immediately started to bark and growl as I approached the gate. It was only when he heard my voice and had a good old sniff at me that the bewildered Butch calmed down and I was able to unlock the gate.

The following morning I arrived at the Studios and I saw this lone huge figure dressed in a long black hooded cape which trailed right down to the ground. He was walking up and down in a most bizarre and ungainly fashion so I decided to get a closer look. By this time the huge figure was sat resting on a chair. As I got closer he stood up and said,

"Good morning".

It was then I realised it was Robert de Niro so I replied,

"Good morning" then mumbled "I never thought you were so tall."

"I'm not, it's these contraptions they put on my feet" he replied in a strong American accent.

At this point he raised the bottom of his cape to reveal he had on a pair of massive long boots with six inch oval shaped soles which gave him a sinister rocking movement when he walked.

"Right" he said, "I'd better get practising in these god darn rocking horse boots they've given me..."

So Robert de Niro continued with his practising and I went off to make-up to have my teeth and spots sorted out.

Incidentally I learnt from the girl in make-up that Robert de Niro had to spend two hours every morning being made up... See it's not easy being a big film star... but still they do get a bit more than eighty quid a day don't they...

Later that day they were rehearsing a fight scene where the character of Frankenstein was to show off his great strength as part of the action. Frankenstein had to pull the driver off his horse and cart and throw him to one side. So in order to get a better view of the action I moved to the front of group of villagers who were watching when the Director shouted.

"Let's go for a take"

One of the villagers behind me said,

"I wouldn't stand there mate, cause when the fight scene starts a body is going to fly past right where you're standing and we are all stunt men and have to take the impact then fall backwards onto the ground."

And that's exactly what happened.

The driver of the horse and cart had a body harness fitted under his clothes which was attached to a hydraulic cable so when Frankenstein threw him off that cart, the cable propelled him through the air into the group of stuntmen who took the impact and fell to the ground giving the impression of Frankenstein's super human strength.

"But don't tell anyone how they did it will you!"

Chapter 27
The Ambulance Man

Another funny moment I had was with that very versatile actor Nigel Havers in a world war two film. The action was he had to parachute out of his plane. Him and his parachute had got caught up in a very large tree. The scene was he had to be cut down, put on a stretcher and taken away by ambulance.

I was to play the part of an ambulance man and the driver, who was also the owner of this pristine 1938 ambulance told me this interesting story. Some thirty five years after the war a farmer had paid him £100 to clear all the junk out of his barn. Among the junk and covered in thirty five years of dust, cobwebs and grime was the 1938 old ambulance. It was restored by the driver back to pristine working condition and was now insured by the film company to the value of £40,000.

But to get back to the story. My instructions were to put the injured Nigel Havers onto a stretcher and into the ambulance. Then I was to close the door and bang on the side of the ambulance which was a signal for the driver to drive off into the distance. We did all that to perfection but I forgot to climb in the ambulance next to Nigel Havers. So after closing the ambulance door dipstick little Teddy Lee banged loud and clear on the side of the ambulance to see it drive away into the distance leaving me stood alone in the wilderness but with the TV crew laughing their heads off behind me.

When we did the retake, this time with me in the ambulance next to the injured and bleeding Nigel Havers, he jokingly said,

"What's going on dear boy! I'm in here doing tragedy and you're out there doing comedy!"

End of story. Well anyway the crew had a good laugh.

So let's get back to the wannabe stuff...

Chapter 28
The Big Fight

I had a phone call from Kerry at Screenlite saying, "Teddy, they've picked you out to be in a soft drink commercial with the boxer Prince Naseem."

My reply, me being a boxing fan was "Great, bring it on".

"It gets better" she said "they also want you to play the part of Prince Naseem's trainer".

So lucky Teddy Lee turned up at Shepperton Studios on a freezing cold morning. It was also very cold in the studio where they had built a mock-up boxing arena with lots of extras to make up the audience. The Director explained the scene to me, that the bell had gone for the end of the round but the two boxers were still fighting...

"At that point Teddy, I want you to get in the ring, grab hold of Prince Naseem and drag him back to his corner."

I thought about this and then said to the Director,

"Does Prince Naseem know I'm going to grab him from behind..." My thinking was the last thing I need is a quick punch in the face from a world champion boxer.

The Director thought for a second and then said,

"Good question Teddy... I'd better go tell him".

I do recall when I did grab him and pull him back to his corner, the man was so fit. The whole of his body was solid muscle. It was like trying to move a huge block of concrete across that boxing ring and back to his corner.

I had several chats with him through the course of the day and found him to be a polite and charming young man. In fact because of the freezing conditions in the studio and his concern for all the extras present, he told the people in charge that something had to be done about it. And as a result, the next morning there were large warm air units all around the studio. So thank you Prince Naseem, lightweight boxing champion of the whole world.

Chapter 29
The Best and the Worst

Right shall Little Teddy Lee tell you about the best looking leading lady I've ever seen...

Or the worst job I've ever done...

Oh all right, the best looking lady!

I'd been given a day's work on a film. The scene was in a small village hall which was full of extras all looking towards a small stage area at the end of the hall where the action was taking place.

From a door at the back in walks the leading lady. She moves along the wall at the side of the hall and stops waiting for her cue to enter the action. If ever a woman turned heads, she did that day. Everything about her was perfect. Her height, figure and looks just seemed to dazzle everyone especially the boys.

We all heard the Director say to his assistant,

"Can you pick out one of the men to be talking to our leading lady as she waits for her cue to enter the action".

The assistant asked me to stand up along with several other lads and said,

"No Teddy, I don't think you're going to be tall enough..."

Needless to say the one he picked out to talk to the beautiful leading lady was gay... there is no justice in this world, is there!

The film was called "Blue Juice" and the leading lady was the very beautiful Catherine Zeta Jones.

And now to the worst job I've ever done. It started with Tony from Ray Knight Agency saying,

"Teddy, that job tomorrow. It's a graveyard scene. Take a dark suit, you're going to be one of the mourners.... Or... they might want you to be a dead body! I'd never played a dead body. I thought that can't be difficult. All you have to do is lay still with your eyes closed.

Anyway on arriving at the shoot I was told,

"You won't need the suit... you're going to be our dead body. Could you go and see the girls in make-up please."

On arriving in make-up I had to strip down to my underpants. They toned down my skin colour to give me a death look. I was given a dressing gown and slippers and then taken to a nearby mortuary.

On arrival the crew were all set up ready to rehearse the scene. I was asked to remove my slippers and dressing gown and lay down on this stainless steel mortuary slab. This I did but the effect of the cold stainless steel slab made me want to go for a pee. On telling the Director this I was told to be quick. So I put on my dressing gown and went to the toilet. Afterwards unfortunately when I turned the tap on to wash my hands, it splashed out all over the front of my light green underpants making it look as if I'd wet myself.

I went back to my cold mortuary slab and quickly covered myself up in the sheet provided without anyone noticing my wet underpants. I heard the Director say,

"Right, let's rehearse this..."

The scene was a mortician and his lady assistant were to enter, roll back the sheet and start to examine the body. On doing this, the actor, who obviously had a good sense of humour, looked at his assistant and said,

"This man's not dead. He's just peed himself..."

Who said playing a dead body was easy...?

Chapter 30
Big Celebrities

Every year in America Bing Crosby used to make a Christmas Special. The last one he ever made was here in England at Elstree Studios. Out on the back lot, they built what I would call a Pickwick type village. Incidentally this same back lot later became the home of "Eastenders" and still is to this very day. That gives you some idea of how long ago it was. Anyway I was given several days work on it.

On the first day I came out of the canteen with a group of extras. One of the girls shouted,

"Look – here's Mr Crosby."

He happily stopped, signed autographs, had his picture taken with some of the girls as if he had all the time in the world. This was a man who had starred in countless Hollywood films and won an Oscar for one of them, which was called "Country Girl" starring the late Grace Kelly.

I had been a fan and enjoyed his music for many years so you can imagine how pleased I was when the next day as I walked by one of the studios I stopped to look inside. At the far end of this empty studio on a small stage was a pianist rehearsing with two men. Unbeknown to them I walked behind the curtained off area and stopped just a few feet away. I don't know who the pianist was but the two men rehearsing a Christmas type song were David Bowie and Bing Crosby! Little did they know that I was just a few feet away peering through those curtains.

A few weeks later I went to the London Palladium to see Bing Crosby and at the start of the show the curtains opened to a darkened stage with just a single spotlight in the centre. Into the spotlight stepped Bing Crosby and every single person in that theatre got to their feet and the applause was deafening... such was the popularity of the man.

The following week he went to Spain and sadly had a fatal heart attack on a golf course there.

But what a good life and a great career this happy and likeable entertainer seemed to enjoy! Thanks for the memories Bing!

Freddie Starr. Most people know he's unpredictable. I had a small part on this TV show "The Freddie Starr Special" There was a scene on a golf course and Freddie had a short putt to make on action. He was supposed to do that but instead he threw his putter to the ground, walked off the green and pretended to have a pee in the bushes. He then turned his head to the cameraman and shouted...

"Do you want to get a close up of my little willy?"

I later spoke to his manager who was also his friend. He told me he went out one morning for a pint of milk and came back with a Rolls Royce limousine. He recalled going for a two week holiday in Spain. They arrived at the hotel, unpacked their bags and the manager went to relax by the pool only to hear Freddie whistle him from the balcony then shout,

"Come on, pack your bags again! We're going home. I don't like this place..."

That's what I call unpredictable!

I remember meeting Billy Connolly, a man whose talent and humour I've always admired. All that I can remember it was a graveyard scene. I was a grave digger and I was stood on a long wooden plank that ran alongside this freshly dug grave. Billy was not in the scene but was stood behind the camera talking to the Director.

The scene ended and I stepped off the wooden plank which caused the side of the freshly dug grave to collapse. I started to slip down into the grave and the only thing that stopped me from finishing up at the bottom of that grave was the long wooden plank which I clung onto dearly. I remember making eye contact with Billy at the time and he gave me one of those "whoopsy daisy" looks.

I got the chance to talk to Billy as he was walking back to his Winnebago. We had both worked in the shipyards and then went into comedy so we had that in common. I don't know what I did for him but he certainly made my day.

"Thanks Billy!"

Chapter 31
Police Matters

I enjoyed driving police cars to and from different locations "The Bill" were filming at. You had to stick a strip of black tape through the word police to let the public know they were not in use. At times you were asked to take some of the extras and actors back to "The Bill" base. On this occasion the Director said,

"Can you take these four men back to base with you Teddy?"

"Yes" I replied, me thinking they were four extras dressed up as policemen... but oh no, they were real coppers so here's Little Teddy Lee happily driving along while talking on my mobile phone, going into a yellow striped junction box when I shouldn't and getting blasted by other road users. My passengers went a bit quiet for a while. It was only when they started talking about Hendon Police College in London, a place where I had performed my act some years earlier, that I thought, Oh Shit, these lads are not extras but real coppers. But they only laughed when I told them I thought they were extras and said,

"Don't worry, we're not going to nick you mate."

I recall when I did perform my act at the Hendon Police College. My younger brother Bill was always happy to come with me on these gigs and act as my unpaid roadie. On this occasion we arrived and Bill went in to check things out while I started to get my speakers and stuff out of the car. I was a bit nervous about performing my act to an all male police audience and got a bit irritated when my brother Bill never came back to help me set up all my gear.

Unbeknown to me, the first person Our Bill spoke to was a Chief Inspector who came from Middlesbrough and he immediately picked up on my brother's Northeast accent and they both got on like a house on fire. The Chief Inspector invited Bill to join him at the top table for a meal. Bill loved his food, especially if it was free... so this was an offer he couldn't refuse. So there was I humping my gear and setting it all up while my roadie was sat at the top table with all the high ranking police dignitaries enjoying a slap up meal...

But it all ended happily because my act went down very well that night. Even though nobody offered me a freebie meal.

Sadly my brother Bill has now passed away along with my mother and all my brothers and sisters with the exception of my younger sister Maureen. She still lives in the Northeast and it is always so nice to visit her and talk about all the good times we have shared together.

I remember doing a small scene with that fine actor John Hurt. He was playing a pervert who was buying sex magazines in a newsagents shop and I was serving behind the counter. I had to watch him enter and select several sex magazines, all with explicit pictures of nude voluptuous young women in different sexual positions. John Hurt was to place the magazines in front of me. I was to look down and determine the price of each one and then tell him the total money he had to pay. The guilty expression on that fine actor's face prompted me to give the exact reaction the Director was looking for because he shouted,

"Cut, we'll buy that! Excellent. Print it. We can release Teddy."

So Little Teddy Lee was wrapped. Finished with a full day's pay and it was only ten o'clock in the morning. All thanks to that fine actor Mr John Hurt.

Another early finish was on the film "Bridget Jones Diary". The location was Tower Bridge. The police had agreed to close the bridge on a Sunday morning from 8 till 10am. The shot the film crew had to get was Bridget Jones walking across a busy Tower Bridge on the way to her office so there were hundreds of extras walking with her and more driving cars, vans etc, just to recreate your typical morning rush hour.

It got to 10am and the uptight Director had asked for more time and the Chief Constable in charge had reluctantly given him another fifteen minutes. When the frustrated Director asked for more time again pointing out the expense the film makers had gone to that morning, the Chief Constable replied,

"And have you any idea Sir, what disruption closing a bridge like this causes to the City of London... so I want you and your people off this bridge... now please!"

When you see the shot in the film, which only lasted a few seconds, you wonder why they both got so uptight about it all... Anyway I had another early finish with more than enough time to enjoy a nice Sunday lunch. Nice one!

The film was "Mission Impossible" starring Tom Cruise. It was a crowded pub scene and we had already been told by the Assistant Director not to make eye contact with Mr Cruise. It was explained he could go anywhere in the world to make his films but he had chosen Britain... so let's make him as comfortable as possible.

So when Tom Cruise walked in the crowded pub, everyone was looking at the wall, ceiling or floor, anywhere but at the man himself. The scene was Tom at one end of the bar watching his supporting actors having a conversation at the other end of the bar. I could see the Assistant Director looking around. He came over to me and said,

"Teddy, I want you to stand at the bar and have a pretend conversation with Mr Cruise..."

Why me? Because Tom's not very tall but stood next to Little Teddy Lee he will look tall.

So the Assistant Director took me over and introduced me to Mr Cruise who looked at me and nodded... so I looked the famous Tom Cruise straight in the eye and nodded back... thinking to myself you don't scare me pal!

I did one day's work on a film called "Wilde" which was about the life and times of the infamous Oscar Wilde. It starred Stephen Fry whose personality and intellect you have to admire.

It was a pretty uneventful day but Stephen Fry tells of the time he stayed in the Savoy Hotel at the same time as Frank Sinatra. The doorman at the hotel said when Mr Sinatra left he gave him a large tip and said,

"I'll bet you've never had a tip as big as that before?"

The doorman looked at the money he'd been given and replied,

"Yes I have Sir."

"Who was that" said the agitated Frank Sinatra, "Come on tell me who was it, come on I want to know who gives bigger tips than me?"

To which the doorman replied,

"It was you Sir... the last time you stayed here!"

So thanks Stephen Fry for sharing that moment with us.

Another job I had was on "Harry Enfield and Chums" and I must say what a nice friendly man he was. I had to play a very powerful military leader who was stood on the stage with his wife, played by the very talented Kathy Burke, who is quite a tall lady. So next to her I didn't look the powerful leader I was supposed to be.

So what did they do?

They stood me on a box, took a head and shoulders shot of us both and bingo... they've got the result they wanted.

"See I told you I was little."

One great occasion in later years was when Gayle, my daughter-in-law gave birth to my beautiful little granddaughter they called Erin.

The first thing I noticed was her gorgeous brown eyes so I just had to write a song about her.

Erin is now seven and she calls me ... Poppa Ted. I've had great fun taking her swimming, teaching her how to ride her bike and watching her grow up and develop into the nice little girl she is today... long may it go on.

Chapter 32
The Best of Laugh of All

I was given a day's work at Pinewood Studios. It was raining heavily when I arrived so I got out of the car and put my head down and my big umbrella up and started to pick my way through the muddy field which was the temporary car park. As I got near the make-up Winnebago with my head still down, there was a clash of brollies. I looked up through the dripping rain, stood in front of me with his brolly up was Mr Sean Connery. I stepped to one side, he nodded politely and walked past.

I was told later by one of the make-up girls that whenever Mr Connery was in the studio he said all the right things, was very polite and created a nice working atmosphere for everyone. This was true because later that day as he was stood on the stage surveying all the village people he spotted me and gave a little nod of recognition. Nice one Mr Connery.

On that same day this incident made me and 500 film extras laugh our heads off. The film was called "First Knight". Richard Gere and Julia Ormond were also starring.

The scene was a village square inside the walls of a medieval castle. At the back of the village square they had built a huge wooden gantry, some twenty feet in height, four feet wide and about 35 yards long. On the floor of the gantry were lots of trapdoors opening and closing, massive gaps you would have to jump across with swords and huge iron balls swinging constantly across your pathway. Add to that lots of sharp iron spikes built into the floor of the gantry.

In the film, the first man to successfully run along this gantry, known as "running the gauntlet" would get to kiss Lady Guinevere, across the other side of the square. Opposite the gantry was a stage with two large high backed chairs for the King and Lady Guinevere. They take their seats in front of the packed village square all excitedly waiting for someone to successfully run the gauntlet and get to kiss the future queen of England.

So in this rehearsal scene, several attempts are made but they all fail. Then up steps Richard Gere as Sir Lancelot dressed in men's tights and ankle boots showing a pair of long legs most women would kill for. Remember this is a man known in the business to have a wicked sense of humour. He'd also had some bad press at the time suggesting he was gay. In fact he and his wife had taken out a full page advert in America stating the opposite. So he successfully completed the gauntlet and is now moving through the crowded village square with everyone chanting,

" Kiss... Kiss... Kiss..."

He reaches the steps that lead up to the stage where the future queen is waiting to be kissed. We see the macho Sean Connery, one hand on his sword, the other reaches out to help Richard Gere up onto the stage. 500 extras are still chanting,

" Kiss... Kiss... Kiss..."

Richard Gere pulls Sean Connery to the floor of the stage and starts to kiss him...

And the whole crowd screamed with laughter.

I must say Sean Connery took it all in good fun and when he got up off the floor, he withdrew his sword and pretended to chop Richard Gere's head off...

So on that happy note, could I just reflect on all my years of being a wannabe and say I've met some very nice and talented people!

I've loved and I've been loved. I have laughed a lot and had the great pleasure of making others laugh. And in my twilight years I am able to see my lovely granddaughter grow up.

All that and I still have the love and care of my beautiful partner Kate.

So I guess you can say I'm a lucky Little Teddy Lee...

THE END

www.ingramcontent.com/pod-product-compliance
Lightning Source LLC
Chambersburg PA
CBHW070306100426
42743CB00011B/2365